A Woman's *Journal*
for Joyful Living

A Woman's *Journal for* Joyful Living

Successful Steps to Holistic Health

Natalie A. Francisco, Ed.D.

Foreword by Dr. Suzan Johnson Cook

A WOMAN'S JOURNAL FOR JOYFUL LIVING: SUCCESSFUL STEPS TO HOLISTIC HEALTH

Cover Photography by RobertoWestbrook.com
Cover Design by Atinad Designs.

© Copyright 2011 by Natalie A. Francisco, Ed. D.

SAINT PAUL PRESS, DALLAS, TEXAS

First Printing, 2011

Unless otherwise noted, the Bible quotations in this volume are from the New King James Version.

The name SAINT PAUL PRESS and its logo are registered as a trademark in the U.S. patent office.

ISBN-13: 978-0-9832651-1-5

Printed in the U.S.A.

DEDICATION

A Woman's Journal for Joyful Living: Successful Steps to Holistic Health is dedicated to the following:

- The single woman who desires to learn from those who have forged a path of successful living for her to follow;

- The teenager, young adult, or woman who has been misused, abused, rejected, neglected, abhorred, or ignored, but yet, is in pursuit of wisdom for a higher level of living;

- The wife who is happily married, in maintenance mode, experiencing difficulty in her marriage, separated, or at the brink of divorce, and has discovered that her own identity and individuality were lost in the process;

- The mother who desires to discover and promote health and wholeness for herself and her children;

- The woman who is an empty-nester with a deep

desire to live a meaningful life of purpose, on purpose;

- Pastor's wives, female clergy and other women in leadership roles who find themselves trying to measure up to the expectations and standards that they or others have set;

- All the past, present, and future *Women of Worth & Worship Institute (WOWWI)* participants and graduates from across the country and around the world whose lives are dedicated to feeding their spirit, mind, and body in ways that cause them to *"prosper and be in health even as [their] souls prosper"* (3 John 2); women who will use their influence to impact their families, communities, nation and world as God's representatives. (Please visit www.NatalieFrancisco.com for more information.)

- This book is dedicated to *you* and your holistic health and the success you seek in every area of your life.

CONTENTS

ACKNOWLEDGEMENTS

First, I give God glory for the many ways He has chosen to teach me valuable lessons via wisdom from His Holy Word, personal experiences, and information observed and gleaned from family, mentors, friends, character builders, and from reading an abundance of resources along my life's journey. I wouldn't trade my life or what I have learned for anything, and have never wanted to trade places with anyone else. I am unapologetically and unequivocally free to be me (and so are you).

To my husband, L. W. Francisco III: I thank you for the determination we both had, and still possess, through the delights and difficulties of balancing marriage, parenthood, entrepreneurship, and ministry for the past twenty-seven plus years. There are many books within us that will require our entire lifetime to write and publish so that others can benefit from what we have learned. Thank you for loving me in your own special way. Know that I love and appreciate you and all I have learned from watching, listening to, and being with you.

To my daughters, Nicole, Lesley, and Lauren: You are the very reason why I have sacrificed so much so that you can soar beyond what we can possibly imagine as women who will impact your generation and the world in profound ways. No mother could be prouder!

To my special "sistah-friends": Michelle McKinney Hammond (Diva), Rev. Connie Jackson (CJ), Rev. Arlicia Albert (Roadie) and Dr. Suzan Johnson Cook (Sujay). God sent you into my life at the exact moment when I needed you the most. I am so very thankful for real sisterhood, void of competition and jealousy, that celebrates our uniqueness, giftedness, and yes, even our silliness. You have brought much needed balance to my life.

To Calvary Community Church (C3) and Calvary Covenant Ministries, Inc.: Thank you for loving our family and being stellar supporters in so many ways. You are the best!

FOREWORD

by Rev. Dr. Suzan Johnson Cook (Dr. Sujay)

Author, *Becoming a Woman of Destiny:*
Turning Trials into Triumphs and *Too Blessed to be Stressed:*
Words of Wisdom for Women on the Move

*I*t was three years ago that I was introduced, by the Rev. Connie "C.J." Jackson, to the author of this profound and timely book, Rev. Natalie Francisco. Rarely, as female leaders in ministry, are we able to find friends and extended family who not only know how to preach, but also LIVE what they preach. I found all of that in Rev. Nat, as we affectionately call her. She has the whole package: family, friends, wholeness in life and in ministry. We were the sister-friends we all longed and looked for all of our lives. So I latched on quickly.

Soon, we were leading one another's services and workshops and being introduced to balanced family and life outside of the pulpit. I was able to see the incredible ministry she had built: Women of Worth and Worship, and found that she could lead such a ministry so effectively because she IS a woman of Great Wisdom and Worth. Thousands of women have been blessed by her leadership and her generous giving.

A Woman's Journal for Joyful Living: Successful Steps to Holistic Health is the compilation of and manifestation of a recent workshop I was privileged to host for international Christian faith leaders: Wisdom Women Worldwide/ Women in Ministry International. It is POWERFUL. I am especially drawn to the first chapter, FREE TO BE ME, because it sets the tone for the book. So many women are spiritually, emotionally, and physically in bondage and don't even know it, or some just need to give themselves permission to be free. Fifteen minutes into the book, you will be captivated and ready to begin to do a personal life assessment. You will be energized. You will be charged and eager to read the remaining chapters.

She is like Mary, a woman who is blessed and highly favored. Her husband is blessed, her children, and her household are all blessed because she is such a blessing to others. And you will find as you read this book that YOU are blessed just by becoming part of her audience.

It is an honor to commend this book to you. May the JOY of the Lord be your strength as you move closer towards JOYFUL LIVING.

INTRODUCTION
by Natalie A. Francisco, Ed.D.

*W*omen throughout the ages have been used to accomplish great things. Despite cultural norms and the opinions of family, friends or foes, we must realize that we were created by God to fulfill a special purpose. No longer can we use the excuses of others to keep us from utilizing our unique gifts and talents in our homes, communities, and work places. Quite often, it is not really the excuses of others that keep us from moving forward in life, but we become the culprit that prevents us from succeeding because we don't take the time to cater to our own spiritual, mental, emotional, and physical wellbeing. For this very reason, I have sensed a mandate to write this book and share its message everywhere I go, in order to mentor women as we administer health and healing to ourselves and others.

God created the physiological and physical anatomy of women so unique as to prove that we can stand the incomprehensible, intense pain and pressure of childbirth and live to tell the story! He created the psychological mentality and personality of women so distinct as to prove that we are multi-faceted, just as a diamond is once it has been refined. Women are empowered to do what needs to be done, albeit taking care of our husband and children, cooking, cleaning, working from or outside of the home, volunteering, attending children's sporting events, recitals and concerts while being the taxi driver, doctor, nurse, teacher, counselor, disciplinarian, and the list goes on and on. However, what we fail to realize is that while we were tending to family members, work, church, and friends' needs, our names and personal interests were never placed on our "to-do" list, and therefore, our own needs were neglected.

Reading and applying the information shared in this book takes nerve as you come face-to-face with your own reality and make the necessary changes to put yourself on your own "to-do" list as a matter of priority. The kind of nerve I am referring to is defined as the mental fortitude and unmitigated audacity to take control of your own life both internally and externally. I challenge you to utilize the mental and moral power within you to transform your present state of mind, spirit, and body into what it was originally designed to be in its best, brightest, and most brilliant form.

I believe that the lessons you are about to encounter will be more than mere words on a page. Rather, the words I share will breathe and breed new life with meaning because you've taken the time and utilized the energy to care for yourself on your journey toward living a joyful, holistically healthy life and lifestyle. Welcome to the path of uncovering and rediscovering the fact that you are a designer's original, specifically created by God with intricate details of spirit, character, and a body frame that was meant to distinguish you from every other person. Your purpose, personality, DNA and fingerprints uniquely identify and separate you from the rest of humanity. So, go ahead—be authentic and celebrate the reality and beauty of yourself and all the endless possibilities of what only you can accomplish. Get ready to discover and climb the steps to successfully reach your destination of holistic health and wholeness. I'll see you at the top!

CHAPTER 1

FREE TO BE ME

*"Because we're God's children, we possess the imprint of
His character and creativity when we recognize and
are energized by who we really are."*
DR. NATALIE A. FRANCISCO

Some would naively think that I have lived a charmed life because of what they may see and perceive from outward appearances at this stage of my life. However, I was not born with a silver spoon in my mouth to wealthy parents and siblings who lived in a prominent neighborhood and always got along with each other like the family from the once popular *Leave It to Beaver* television show from the 1950s and 1960s era, or *The Cosby Show* from the 1980s. I did not attend private schools, or receive life handed to me on a silver platter, while being protected from the hard knocks and grueling task master of life, and from some of the people who simply rubbed me the wrong way. Yet, I still lived an incredibly blessed life and never lacked anything, especially as the baby girl of the family.

I would later learn that the most difficult experiences of

life would become my most valuable lessons, and that the people least likely to be granted entrance into my life at my own invitation would become my greatest character builders in my journey towards uncovering and discovering who I really am, apart from my immediate and extended family, as well as what I would accomplish. Perhaps you can relate to my story as well.

Some of us never make the leap from being defined by our family or occupation to embracing who we are apart from both entities, and some may prefer to stay in that paradigm. However, I believe there are others who refuse to be solely defined by another person, an occupation, a vocation, or by society's status quo of who we should become, how we should look, and with whom we should associate. If that statement alone resonates with you, then keep reading!

There are countless women who live as though their lives are a silent movie playing on a screen, but without a message that can be heard because they have hidden their unique voice, and therefore, have masked their authentic selves. Some men may fall into this category as well because they, too, have allowed others to speak on their behalf and make decisions for them rather than taking the reins to control their own life and choose for themselves. Many young people fall prey to peer pressure and are in the same situation of following instead of leading, sometimes being bullied by others to fit in with the crowd rather than choosing to boldly stand up and stand out in the midst of the crowd.

Oh, yes, there are adults who are still succumbing to that kind of pressure, albeit on a more advanced scale.

I survived growing up in a neighborhood that would encounter increasingly worsening conditions, and attending public school and college littered with the lure of drugs, alcohol, promiscuity and many people with an identity crisis. I learned through the experiences of dealing with all kinds of people and situations that it is important to have a belief system and a moral code by which to live that would guide my thoughts and actions. That belief system was introduced to me first by my parents, and in particular by my mother, who instilled a love for and a fear of God in me as a young child. Later in life, I would develop a desire to utilize biblical principles as my moral code and compass to both lead me in making the right decisions and convict me when I've made wrong choices on my quest of discovering the real me.

I must admit that my first encounter with the mirror of life occurred when I was in the seventh grade of what was then known as C. Vernon Spratley Junior High School. Up until that point, I had allowed myself to be bullied by one particular girl from kindergarten all the way through sixth grade. I would later find out that her older sister bullied my oldest sister when she was in grammar school. Our mother had always taught us to "turn the other cheek" as good Christian girls and that is literally what we had done. But it took one look in the mirror of the girls' restroom at

Spratley for me to realize that I deserved to be treated better and to live better than that!

I'll never forget that day. After washing my hands in the basin and proceeding to exit the girls' restroom, I caught a glimpse of myself in the full length mirror. The way I walked, looked and dressed reflected how I felt and thought of myself at the time. My eyes were slightly downcast, and I had heard from the neighborhood bully, from the time I was five years old until I turned twelve, that I looked Chinese as she taunted me with name calling and jeers on the walk home from school each day. My parents decided to drive me to school, but that didn't stop the bullying. I walked with uncertainty and insecurity as I noticed how my shoulders slumped and my feet were carelessly turned outward while walking toward the mirror next to the restroom door. Although I had now heard from both girls and boys alike at Spratley how beautiful my eyes were, I didn't believe them because I lacked the confidence to believe in myself. The ridiculing words I'd heard had plagued me for so long that I chose to believe what the bully said about me as "truth" even though it wasn't "the truth" (as my daughter Lesley would say). When I saw my image in the mirror that day, I knew without anyone else telling me that I needed to change and be changed. The girls' restroom became my transformation chamber that day.

I made a conscious decision soon thereafter to change the

way I thought and spoke about myself. I began to dress, act, walk, and talk differently, and I began to choose to be around those who appreciated and celebrated me rather than those who berated or hated me. I even came up with my own signature hair style—the mushroom! I began to see myself as successful, even though I was always an honor roll student. Everyone noticed the difference in me, but not as much as I did. When walking in the cafeteria and traversing through the lunch line, I was mistaken for a teacher and given a teacher's lunch many times as a result. Even the bully noticed a change after I stood up for myself and fought back. And that was the end of her days of harassing me!

I believe that God allowed my eyes to be opened when I looked in that mirror of life, not just physically, but spiritually, mentally, and emotionally as well. That was the first of many encounters I had to remind me that others do not, and should never be, allowed to define me. I discovered that some people may say or do hurtful things because "hurting people hurt other people" (as Joyce Meyer would say). The bully who taunted me, as well as others who said and did cruel things, either intentionally or unintentionally, were actually character builders who made me stronger. It took the trials rather than the triumphs of life to transform me into who I am today.

My most beloved passages of scripture are Jeremiah 1:5-8 and 29:11-13, and Psalm 139:13-18. Consider the lessons

Jeremiah and David learned in the verses below from the New King James Version. Upon further examination of these passages, we can extrapolate reliable principles from which we can learn and apply to our lives.

Jeremiah 1:5-8:

"Before I formed you in the womb I knew you; Before you were born I sanctified you; I ordained you a prophet to the nations."

Then said I: "Ah, Lord GOD! Behold, I cannot speak, for I am *a youth."*

But the LORD said to me: "Do not say, 'I am a youth,' For you shall go to all to whom I send you, And whatever I command you, you shall speak.

Do not be afraid of their faces, For I am *with you to deliver you," says the LORD.*

Application Principles

1. ***God knew us before we were born.*** In Jeremiah 1:5, God tells Jeremiah that He knew of and about him before his parents conceived him. Isn't that awesome to think about? Apparently, this verse implies that there is not just an "after life" to be concerned about, but that there was a "before life" also as reiterated by the fact that Jeremiah was in God's presence before he was an embryo or a fetus.

Now I believe that because God said this to Jeremiah, it applies to us as well. We need to realize that the essence of who we really are is not the physical image that we see in the mirror, but it is the spirit that gives life to our body as God originally designed.

2. *We were designed with a specific purpose in mind.* Verse five lets us know that we weren't created by chance. God told Jeremiah that he was sanctified (or distinctly set apart) to be a prophet (a spokesperson for God) to the nations. Jeremiah, and every other creation of God, was created to fulfill a particular purpose for a reason in a specific season. No birth was or is a mistake, no matter how horrendous the circumstances were or are. We must embrace that God had a distinct purpose in mind for each of us.

3. *We all feel inadequate and fearful at times, but that should not be used as an excuse for refusing to move forward.* In verses six and seven, Jeremiah has a discourse with God about his feelings of insecurity and inadequacy because of his youthfulness and inexperience. However, God quickly responds by emphasizing that Jeremiah is not alone and that a change needs to take place, starting with the way Jeremiah viewed and spoke about himself. Low self-esteem and a poor self-image would not serve Jeremiah or his purpose very

well, and the same is true for us. Consequently, we must choose to open our spiritual and natural eyes to see ourselves as the beautiful inner spirit and outer masterpiece that God designed. When we accept that as our personal truth, then we will be transformed.

4. *Fear must take a backseat to our destiny.* In verse eight, God further responds to Jeremiah by telling him not to be afraid of others' faces, for God alone would be Jeremiah's source of strength and deliverer. Jeremiah didn't even know he needed to be delivered, not just from those who would oppose him, but from his own faulty thinking, and the same principle can be applied to us. We need not fear the disapproving looks, thoughts, or comments of others, or the disparaging opinions that we have of ourselves. Faith in God will remove fear from the driver's seat and place it behind us where it belongs. That is not to say that we will never be fearful in the future. In fact, fear can serve as a reminder that our sufficiency and dependency is to be in God rather than in our human abilities alone.

Jeremiah 29:11-13:

> *For I know the thoughts that I think toward you, says the LORD, thoughts of peace and not of evil, to give you a future and a hope.*

Then you will call upon Me and go and pray to Me, and I will listen to you.
And you will seek Me and find Me, when you search for Me with all your heart.

Application Principles

1. ***God is thinking about and desires the best for us.*** God reiterates to Jeremiah in chapter 29 verse 11 that He *knows* him, which implies both present and ongoing thought and deliberation about everything that concerns Jeremiah's purpose and wellbeing. His best interest was on the mind and heart of God, and so is ours. We need to accept that God both knows and wants what is best for us, and that is why it is imperative that we take time to know God and His plans for us (rather than just our own). The events and experiences of our past, present, and future can be used by God for a greater purpose to promote peace, health, wholeness and hope for ourselves and others.

2. ***Communicating with God connects us to the source of all wisdom and strength.*** It is not until Jeremiah desires to know God's plan for his life that he realizes he must actively pursue a relationship with God through prayer. God emphatically states in verses 12 and 13 that He will listen to Jeremiah when he

calls upon Him and searches for God with his whole heart. Herein is the difference between religion and a relationship. A religious experience is encountering God based on what others mandate— perhaps the observance of learned behavior or a set of rules, regulations and rites of passage that are required. On the contrary, a relationship is the mutual exchange of authentic, honest communication between ourselves and God so that prayer is not just an observance during a particular time, but becomes a conversation that is not just verbal, but intellectual and emotional throughout the day as both the mind and the heart are engaged with and connected to the One who has all of the answers to the vicissitudes of life. Prayer, then, is a life-giving force that maintains and sustains us while we pursue holistic health and purpose.

Psalm 139:13-18:

For You formed my inward parts; You covered me in my mother's womb.

I will praise You, for I am fearfully and wonderfully made; Marvelous are Your works,

And that my soul knows very well.

My frame was not hidden from You, When I was made in secret, And skillfully wrought in the lowest parts of the earth.

Your eyes saw my substance, being yet unformed.
And in Your book they all were written,
  The days fashioned for me, When as yet there
were none of them.
  How precious also are Your thoughts to me, O God!
How great is the sum of them!
  If I should count them, they would be more in
number than the sand; When I awake, I am still
with You.

Application Principles

1. ***Everything about us is intentionally unique and wonderful.*** In Psalm 139, David, who was a shepherd boy, giant slayer, musician, and king of Israel, declares some of the lessons learned by being in the presence of God in prayerful meditation. In verses 13-15, he realizes that God knew and formed him, just as He did Jeremiah, before He was placed in his mother's womb. The confidence of David is beautifully illustrated as he boldly penned that he was *"fearfully and wonderfully made; marvelous are Your [God's] works, and that my soul [mind, will, intellect, emotions and imagination] knows very well."* (I added the phrases in italics and brackets.) Notice that the confidence David portrays is rooted in what God has done and created and not in arrogance or selfish ambition. It is perfectly fine to

boast in who God is and what He has done and is doing in and through us, which is the distinguishing difference between confidence and conceit.

2. *Every detail and day of our lives has been seen and hand-written by God.* Nothing escapes the all-seeing eye of God. He is Omnipresent (All-Present), Omniscient (All-Knowing) and Omnipotent (All-Powerful), which means He is everywhere we will ever go, is aware of everything we need to know, and is the source of all the strength we could possibly need to live a life above the status quo. He is not surprised by what happens to or around us, because His plans are always for our good. (Read Jeremiah 29:11 and Romans 8:28.) Our part in the plan of God is to stop worrying and start trusting in God and what He desires to accomplish in and through us, and that is a daily choice.

3. *God is always thinking of us and His thoughts are what matter the most.* In verses 17 and 18, David has discovered the same revelation as Jeremiah: God is thinking of him even during the times when David isn't necessarily thinking of God. It's mind boggling to imagine that we are in God's thoughts temporally and eternally while we sleep, pray, eat, work, play, and even falter along the way. What we do does not cancel God's original assignment for

us or His thoughts about us. Here is some food for thought: we can never earn God's love or approval. It was already given before we were born and extended to us through grace, mercy, and the gift of life that we experience when we open our hearts to God and live for Him instead of ourselves. That is the most important decision we could ever make.

I learned through life's experiences as a child, teenager, musician, worship leader, young wife and mother, college/ graduate student, entrepreneur, pastor's wife, teacher, principal, administrator, Bible college professor, ordained minister, co-pastor, and author (Whew...and the list continues!), that my personality, gifts, talents, and abilities were given so that I could be the person God originally intended. I have felt unbelievable pressure to look, talk, dress, and conduct myself like someone else, but at the same time to be true to who I am meant to be—that is, genuine, transparent, and free from the opinions and expectations of others. I am free to be me, and you are free to be you (if you will accept that freedom). My good friend, Arlicia, would put it this way: "You do you and let me do me!" There's no greater person for you or me to be.

Where Do I Go From Here?
Accountability and Responsibility Journaling

- Sometimes, a major event or experience in our past can cause our sense of self-value and worth to be diminished. Has that happened to you, and if so, what was the event or experience as you remember it? How did it shape you into the person you are now?

  _____

  _____

  _____

  _____

  _____

  _____

  _____

- When and what was your first encounter with "the mirror of life" that caused you to seek after and make a change in the way you perceived yourself?

  _____

  _____

  _____

  _____

  _____

  _____

- Nine application principles from the lives of Jeremiah and David were shared for reflection as we examined Jeremiah 1:5-8 and 29:11-13, and Psalm 139:13-18. Which ones do you identify with the most? List them below and utilize your journal to develop a strategy to apply each principle to your life within a specified time-frame.

_____

_____

_____

_____

_____

_____

_____

CHAPTER 2

THE PEOPLE PLEASER PERSONALITY

"I don't know the key to success, but the key to failure is trying to please everyone."
BILL COSBY

Once we learn that we are free to be who we really are (and that the decision to do so has always been ours to make), it is equally important to realize that we cannot be all things to all people. In fact, it is humanly impossible and utterly absurd to take on the weight of that responsibility, for it will do seemingly irreparable damage to us and those closest to us. No one's shoulders can carry that oversized burden, so why should we try?

In chapter seven of my first book, *Wisdom for Women of Worth and Worship: Lessons for a Life of Virtue, Value and Victory*, I wrote about the Superwoman Syndrome. Let me expand upon that by sharing that many of us have taken the lyrics of Alicia Keyes' song, "Superwoman," literally and have gotten others to join in the hype: *"'Cause I am a superwoman, yes I am. (Yes she is.) Still when I'm a mess, I still put on a vest with an 'S' on my chest. Oh yes, I'm a superwoman."* I used to think that I had to be that woman because it was expected of me, but the truth made me free!

The truth is this, and I challenge you to read it aloud to hear it come from your own lips: *Since I cannot be all things to all people, I do not have to pretend to be someone or something that I am not for the sake of pleasing people.* Now, didn't it sound good to hear those words proclaimed from your own mouth? In fact, the profundity of that statement is worth repeating: *Since I cannot be all things to all people, I do not have to pretend to be someone or something that I am not for the sake of pleasing people.*

Let's take this truth a step further. When we stand before God to give an account for our lives and the gifts He gave us, do you think that our husbands (for those of us who are married), significant others, children, family, church members, co-workers, friends or foes will stand to answer for us? The answer is emphatically NO! We each must individually face either the judgment seat of Christ, if we have accepted Jesus as our personal Savior and Lord, or the great white throne, if we choose to reject Him. The bottom line is our life is not about pleasing people, but about pleasing God. (For personal study regarding this, read Hebrews 4:13 and 13:17 as well as I Peter 4:5; Romans 14:10; 2 Corinthians 5:10 and Revelation 20:11-13.)

In the early days of ministry, I must admit that I was

enamored, enthralled, and yet obstructed and overwhelmed, by the expectations and the role of a pastor's wife. Who was she, and what was she to do? There was no list of responsibilities or job description given, so I was left to discover the answer to those questions and more to follow by observing other women, such as my dear mother-in-law, who was also a pastor's wife and others in the community who fit the description. From my observations, the expectations were to be publicly self-deprecating, submissive no matter what, quiet, opinion-less, impeccably dressed, poised and polished, with an unwavering desire to promote the pastor's vision (that is, if there was a vision) while meeting the needs in the church (especially when others wouldn't step up to the plate), in the midst of balancing the roles of marriage, motherhood, and ministry. And yes, you guessed it…that was during the time when I thought I had to be Superwoman to meet the expectations of others. That kind of pressure is unfair, unrealistic, unfathomable, and unhealthy.

No one imposed those expectations on me. I placed them on myself based on what I saw and heard in religious circles. It wasn't until about six years ago (when I turned forty) that I had a series of epiphanies that would cause me to think unconventionally about church and religiosity versus relationship. A relationship with God frees us from the presuppositions and presumptions defined by religious doctrines and learned behavior, and replaces religion with the pursuit of God, His purpose and our passion.

Pastor's wives and female clergy aren't the only ones who sometimes buy into the Superwoman Syndrome. Homemakers, single women, entrepreneurs, divorcees, widows, and women from all socio-economic walks of life are meandering in a malaise of mistreatment of their own body, mind, and spirit because others' needs and expectations have, for far too long, taken precedence over their own. For that reason, many suffer from physical illness, emotional burnout and mental exhaustion, particularly in the African-American community as women have had to take on the enormity of responsibilities, both in and outside of the home, out of necessity, without managing their life and time properly, scheduling annual check-ups with a physician or receiving professional therapy/counseling when needed. The personal pursuit of holistic health and wholeness has never been placed on the "to-do list" of priorities.

Now, there are some who would argue that putting one's own needs ahead of others is selfish and unbiblical. I strongly disagree. In fact, Jesus tells us to love our neighbor as we love ourselves in the gospels of Matthew, Mark and Luke. We can surmise from this admonition that we cannot adequately or fully love and care for our neighbor unless we have first learned how to love and care for ourselves. We will address this topic in chapter five (Practicing Self-Care).

I must also add that loving our neighbor does not mean

that we are to become a push over or a door mat to be used at their discretion. There is another side of love, often referred to as *tough love*, that may be needed in order to point the way to Jesus as their source, rather than us, so that we do not become people pleasers or enablers. There is one simple word that must become a regular part of our vocabulary in order to avoid the people pleaser personality, which can easily cause us to become overburdened with tasks and responsibilities that perhaps our neighbor should carry, and that simple word is "no". To become comfortable with using this word and really meaning it, practice saying it in the mirror if necessary while paying attention to body language and voice inflections. Others will be able to tell if we are serious when we respond to them based on how this simple word is communicated, and whether or not we back up our response with our intended display of tough love. Remember that our goal is not to please people, but to please our audience of one—God.

There was a man by the name of Saul in the Old Testament who, despite the fact that God had chosen him to be king of Israel at the Israelites' request, was more concerned about pleasing people than he was about pleasing God. In the beginning verses of I Samuel chapter 15, God told the prophet Samuel to instruct Saul to utterly destroy the Amalekites who were enemies of Israel. Saul was not to leave anything alive, not even the sheep! But Samuel soon discovered that Saul had disobeyed God's original command for the sake of pleasing and looking good in the eyes of the people he was called to lead. God was upset with Saul, and as a result, led the prophet Samuel to replace Saul by anointing David as Israel's new king – a man who pursued and gained the heart of God.

Let's delve into the scriptural passage below and uncover principles that can be applied to our own lives.

I Samuel 15:24-30:

Then Saul said to Samuel, "I have sinned, for I have transgressed the commandment of the LORD and your words, because I feared the people and obeyed their voice.

Now therefore, please pardon my sin, and return with me, that I may worship the LORD."

But Samuel said to Saul, "I will not return with you, for you have rejected the word of the LORD, and the LORD has rejected you from being king over Israel."

And as Samuel turned around to go away, Saul seized the edge of his robe, and it tore.

So Samuel said to him, "The LORD has torn the kingdom of Israel from you today, and has given it to a neighbor of yours, who is better than you.

And also the Strength of Israel will not lie nor relent. For He is not a man, that He should relent."

Then he said, "I have sinned; yet honor me now, please, before the elders of my people and before

Israel, and return with me, that I may worship the LORD your God."

Application Principles

1. ***God's approval of and instructions for our lives supersedes that of others.*** It is apparent in verse 24 that Saul feared the people in his kingdom. He was controlled by their whims and wishes, and therefore, he had abdicated his throne without even knowing it. Instead of leading the nation of Israel, he assumed the position of following them. Good leadership requires wisdom, knowledge, understanding, and counsel from a source higher and greater than one's self. Having mentors and aspiring to learn from exceptional leaders is commendable, but the greatest Leader of all time is God who knows our calling, character, and capabilities and can lead us in the right direction when we allow Him to do so.

2. ***It is best to "fess up" when we "mess up."*** Saul asked Samuel to forgive him for not following God's original instructions in verse 25, but notice that he only confessed after he was confronted. So many people fall into this category, only asking to be forgiven after being caught rather than being up front about the indiscretion or infraction on their

own. The lesson to be learned here is certainly to ask for forgiveness when we have missed the mark from God and individuals that are affected by our wrong decisions and/or actions.

3. *Doing the right thing for the right reason will yield the right results.* Saul obviously was more concerned with impressing people than he was of following God's directives as we can see in verses 26-30, and the consequences for him were disastrous. When we seek to do what is right, and use the resources within us and at our disposal to do so with a spirit of excellence, then we can expect good results to follow. We are who we are, and do what we do, not to make ourselves look good, but to live in such a way that God's light shines through us for a greater purpose.

I had the pleasure of meeting a wonderful woman by the name of Dr. Marian L. Heard through our mutual friend, Dr. Suzan Johnson Cook. We toured the White House together and have had the pleasure of being in the same circles to influence and empower women. Marian is a woman whose leadership has garnered the recognition of six U.S. Presidents who have valued her input and expertise. She knows who she is and what she has to offer, as can be quickly assessed by being in her presence. Although she has great love and admiration for people and the work that she does (and by her own admission, she has ten different streams of income), she has not sailed uncharted waters and achieved unparalleled success by trying to please people, but rather, by living in such an excellent manner that she pleases God.

In Marian's book, *The Complete Leader: Your Path to the Top*, she shares the following quote by Thomas Wentworth Higginson: "Do not waste a minute—not a second—in trying to demonstrate to others the merits of your performance. If your work does not vindicate itself, you cannot vindicate it." I couldn't have stated it better.

Where Do I Go From Here?
Accountability and Responsibility Journaling

- Is there a person whose favor or approval you are desperately seeking? If so, whom, and why do you believe you need it?

  _____

  _____

  _____

  _____

  _____

  _____

- The Message Bible translation of Proverbs 16:7 states, "When God approves of your life, even your enemies will end up shaking your hand." Does your mindset need to change concerning how you view yourself and interact with others now that you know God already approves of you and will cause those who don't to find favor with you? If so, list two things you will do to transform your thinking in light of Proverbs 16:7.

  _____

  _____

  _____

  _____

_____

_____

_____

- Write down the names of the people you have tried to impress or please, both past and present. How will you change this pattern of behavior in the immediate future?

  _____

  _____

  _____

  _____

  _____

  _____

CHAPTER 3

I CAN RUN BUT I CAN'T HIDE

*"Each one of us has to find his peace from within.
And peace, to be real, must be unaffected by
outside circumstances."*
GANDHI

One of the many hats I've worn (literally) and continue to wear (figuratively) is that of a pastor's wife. I remember being the first to arrive to church and the last to leave along with my husband for many years, especially in the early days of ministry. I carried responsibilities without a title or compensation for years, and received no accolades and very little recognition for all that was done behind the scenes. There were days when I wore a smile on my face while I felt like screaming and running away because of how I was spoken to and treated by some people. But I soon discovered that even if I did run, I could not hide, especially from God. He knew what I was really thinking and feeling behind my smile, rhinestone trimmed suit and matching hat with coordinated stilettos!

Mahatma Gandhi wisely stated that "each one of us has to

find his peace from within. And peace, to be real, must be unaffected by outside circumstances." How profound to realize that peace cannot be obtained from external people, places or things. Instead, unlimited peace can be accessed from the well of our own spirit as we seek to connect with God on a daily basis. Isn't that good to know?

There are many who have not learned that lesson, and therefore seek peace via the escape mechanisms of alcohol, prescription and illegal drug use, promiscuity, other people, overspending, overworking, overeating, and other addictive behaviors. The reason for succumbing to the allure of these addictions stems from a need to avoid rather than confront the realities that may exist. It is much easier for some to live in a world of oblivion than to actually deal with the root cause of what has gone wrong and why.

I must note that often times, church can be used as a means of escape as well. Marriages and families have suffered as a result of one or both spouses spending more time in the pew volunteering than in their home with each other and their children, and pastors and their families are not excluded from this group. This is is why I have dedicated an entire section of this book to "Prioritizing Family and Others" in chapter 7. It is no wonder why many young people who once spent more time in the back pews in church services than they did at home doing homework and spending quality time with their parents and siblings, end up leaving church, sometimes never to return, as their method of escape.

I also serve as the Minister of Music and worship leader in my local church, and have loved doing so for more than 25 years. During that time, I have led the congregation in exuberant praise and reverent worship, only to realize that praise and worship can also be thought of and used by some as a place to run and hide while releasing pent-up emotions and seeking refuge from what is still waiting after the benediction has ended. God is indeed a strong tower to whom we can run and find safety, especially when we need Him the most, but He is not to be thought of as some cosmic genie that will make all of our wishes come true when offering up a song, dance, shout or tithe. That is not the reason for connecting with Him through prayer or acts of worship. Rather, we connect with Him because we recognize that we need Him to guide, direct and influence our decisions so that our life will please Him and impact others for a greater purpose.

Coming to and participating in church alone will not change a person's spiritual, physical, economic or social condition, but genuinely connecting with God and utilizing sound biblical principles to influence our daily thoughts, words and actions will transform us from the inside out and manifest real peace. External issues can only be addressed and resolved when they are proactively confronted rather than swept under the carpet to be ignored. As they say, "Out of sight, out of mind!" Then again, that statement provides no solution whatsoever. It only serves as an excuse to run and hide.

Running and hiding is not a novel idea, although it certainly will not provide the answer for any of life's challenges. But don't just take my word for it. Let's take a look at a biblical example of this escape mechanism as used by Gideon in the Old Testament book of Judges.

Judges 6:11-16:

> Now the Angel of the LORD came and sat under the terebinth tree which was in Ophrah, which belonged to Joash the Abiezrite, while his son Gideon threshed wheat in the winepress, in order to hide it from the Midianites.
>
> And the Angel of the LORD appeared to him, and said to him, "The LORD is with you, you mighty man of valor!"
>
> Gideon said to Him, "O my lord, if the LORD is with us, why then has all this happened to us? And where are all His miracles which our fathers told us about, saying, 'Did not the LORD bring us up from Egypt?' But now the LORD has forsaken us and delivered us into the hands of the Midianites."
>
> Then the LORD turned to him and said, "Go in this might of yours, and you shall save Israel from the hand of the Midianites. Have I not sent you?"

So he said to Him, "O my Lord, how can I save Israel? Indeed my clan is *the weakest in Manasseh, and I* am *the least in my father's house."*

And the LORD said to him, "Surely I will be with you, and you shall defeat the Midianites as one man."

Application Principles

1. ***Our natural talents and abilities are not to be hidden but exist to display God's strength operating through us.*** In verse 11, the Angel of the Lord appeared to Gideon to bring clarity and correction to his perception of himself. Gideon was hiding in the winepress, a place that was meant to be used to crush grapes in order to extract juice for the purpose of making wine. Gideon, because of his fear of people (in particular, the Midianites who oppressed Israel at the time), was hiding there to thresh wheat, a process used to separate the seed of the wheat from the straw, chaff, husks and other residue. Ironically enough, Gideon was about to learn a lesson in threshing that would separate what he thought of himself from God's thoughts about him and purpose for him. Gideon was in the wrong place (winepress), doing the wrong thing (threshing wheat).

2. ***God is with us even when we think He is not.*** In verse 12, the Angel told Gideon that God was with

him and that he was a mighty man of valor (strength, courage and nerve), even though his actions proved that Gideon thought the opposite. Other synonyms for valor include bravery, spirit, gallantry, fearlessness and boldness. Those traits are not germane to men alone. Women need to know that we are mighty in valor and virtue as well, and that we have innate qualities and gifts that have been hidden for far too long. Accepting that God is with us musters up boldness to show what He can do through vessels willing to excel in His strength.

3. *God sends us to the people who are in our sphere of influence on purpose.* In verses 13 and 14, God reiterates that Gideon was sent by Him to conquer the very people he was hiding from because of fear. That was certainly news to Gideon, and it may be news for you, too! Consider this: You are where you are, doing what you are doing, for a reason. Even the enemies in your life (or as some call, "the haters") are character builders strategically placed in your presence to bring out the best in you that you never thought or knew existed. God can use those who are against you to propel you into your purpose.

4. *Magnifying our familial or personal weaknesses is unproductive, but magnifying God yields winning results.* In verse 15, Gideon blamed his

lack of productivity on his family, upbringing and once again, on his perceived weaknesses. However, that was no excuse for not producing the results of which he was capable. God quickly emphasized, once again, that Gideon was not alone and that the Lord was with Him to defeat the Midianites "as one man" in verse 16. It is interesting to note that the strength of God dwelling inside of us is more than an innumerable host of human harnessed power around us. With that knowledge, how could Gideon lose? He was a winner before he ever fought a battle, and so are we!

As the above passage regarding Gideon illustrates, there is really no place to run or hide from the presence of God. He sees and knows all about us, and is with us even when we least feel Him. There is no mountain too high, valley too low or river too wide that could overwhelm or overflow us if we turn inward and upward in our search for peace and wisdom to handle the affairs of life no matter how difficult they may seem. God is the ultimate shelter where we can hide, for when we run to Him, He will remind us that *"No temptation has overtaken you except such as is common to man; but God is faithful, who will not allow you to be tempted beyond what you are able, but with the temptation will also make the way of escape, that you may be able to bear it"* (1 Corinthians 10:13). Simply put, we are not alone in what we experience in life. Others have gone through and will go through the same ordeal, which makes it commonplace. God is with us and knows exactly how much we can handle. All that is beyond us needs to be released to God as well as delegated to others as necessary.

Where Do I Go From Here?
Accountability and Responsibility Journaling

- Have you ever felt an overwhelming desire to run and hide from life? Describe the experience and what caused you to feel that way. To what or whom did you turn to avoid facing reality?

  _____

  _____

  _____

  _____

  _____

  _____

- With the knowledge you now have after reading this chapter, how would you respond differently to the situation described above?

  _____

  _____

  _____

  _____

  _____

  _____

- Psalm 46:1-5 in the Message Bible offers hope by

reminding us that, "God is a safe place to hide, ready to help when we need him. We stand fearless at the cliff-edge of doom, courageous in seastorm and earthquake. Before the rush and roar of oceans, the tremors that shift mountains. Jacob-wrestling God fights for us. River fountains splash joy, cooling God's city, this sacred haunt of the Most High. God lives here, the streets are safe, God at your service from crack of dawn." With this in mind, list an issue (if applicable) that is confronting you right now and is too overwhelming for you to handle. What will you do in an effort to hide *in God* rather than in people, places or things?

_____

_____

_____

_____

_____

_____

_____

CHAPTER 4

LOVING AND FORGIVING

"There are only three things you need to let go of: judging, controlling, and being right. Release these three and you will have the whole mind and twinkly heart of a child."
HUGH PRATHER

There are many things I have learned and know for sure, and one of them is that I must walk in love and forgive, even when I don't feel like it. After all, love does cover a multitude of sins and faults, and the greater the love we have for others, the smaller their shortcomings will become. Jesus is the perfect portrait of love and forgiveness based on what He said when His accusers hung Him on a cross after being ridiculed, spat upon, bruised and beaten. He said, *"Father, forgive them, for they do not know what they do"* (Luke 23:24).

That doesn't mean that we should totally ignore the actions of persons that prove detrimental to our mental, emotional and/or physical wellbeing. There is no excuse for those who batter and abuse others in any way, shape or form. Jesus became the ultimate sacrifice by taking on the sins of the entire world, so there is no need to sacrifice ourselves by allowing others to mistreat and misuse us. Abuse of any kind is reprehensible and should not be tolerated in any relationship, friendship or association. Every human being deserves to be treated with dignity and respect which must be given if it is to be gained.

We are to forgive others not so much for their sakes, but for ours. Refusing to forgive causes resentment, bitterness and anger to develop which hurts the person who harbors those feelings more than the offender, who goes along life merrily as if he or she could care less. However, releasing the offender and placing them in the hands of God takes strength of character and commitment. Doing so will free our mind, spirit and body in such a way that allows God to heal the hurts and scars that are hidden to others but openly revealed to Him.

In order to truly forgive, we must seek to truly love without preconceived conditions. Unconditional love is not based on what a person does or does not do, but rather on a choice to love in spite of what a person does or does not do. There is an entire chapter in the Bible dedicated to the subject of love in 1 Corinthians 13 that we should read and meditate upon often, especially when we need to demonstrate more love toward others. To paraphrase the chapter, Paul shows us that love sees the good and not the evil, the intentions rather than the expectations, and the best instead of the worst. Doesn't that sound like what couples pledge to do when they say their wedding vows: "to love and to honor, and to be true to one another for better or for worse, for richer or for poorer, in sickness or in health, 'til death us do part"? These are vows that should be committed to and taken seriously between husbands and wives.

The divorce rate in the U.S. continues to escalate as more and more couples refuse to honor their commitments because of what society excuses as irreconcilable differences. Separation, divorce and remarriage have become a matter of convenience and popularity according to our culture because love and forgiveness are downplayed, and so is the institution of marriage.

In the opening quote of this chapter, Hugh Prather stated that there are three things we need to let go of in order to have a pure heart like that of a child: "...judging, controlling, and being right." Now, I don't know about you, but for me, that is a mouthful! It is much easier for me to see and quickly point out what is wrong because of my personality. I am the kind of person who can walk into a room and easily assess what needs to be done more effectively and efficiently and by whom. I often read books published by others and my eyes naturally find the grammatical and mechanical errors without looking for them. I'm also a teacher by nature, and as such, find myself often offering correction whether or not it was solicited...and I have a daughter who is just like me. Heaven help us!

I confess that I have some perfectionist tendencies, but I have submitted that area to God and am working even now to strive for excellence which is attainable rather than perfection which is impossible in this life in my pursuits as well as in my dealings with others and vice versa. To avoid the frustration that comes with possessing perfectionist tendencies, I am learning to embrace the freedom that comes with striving to accomplish every endeavor to the best of my abilities with the resources I have. Perhaps you can relate. I know I'm not the only one who needs to give up control, become less critical, and admit that I'm not always right. If that doesn't fit you, I'm sure it fits someone you know. Tell the truth now!

Letting go of the need to control and judge others and to always be right requires compromising and seeing from another person's point of view with empathy. This attitude of the mind, heart and will can mend relationships within homes, churches, workplaces, communities and even nations as we seek to do so for the mutual benefit of the parties involved. Loving and forgiving those who offend, especially those with whom we share our lives, is a necessity. Doing so honors God and ensures that He forgives us of our trespasses as well.

There are some who might say, "I can forgive and have forgiven, but I'll never forget." I can identify with that statement because I have an incredible memory. Even the things I want to forget stick with me like white on rice! It is more difficult for those like me to forget, whereas others, like my husband, can easily forgive because he can't remember why he was offended or who was the offender in the first place. My mind works more like a computer that easily retrieves data at warp speed. Believe me, I do understand that it is not as easy to forget when you are detail-oriented and can see in your mind's eye the offender(s), what they were wearing, what was said and how it was communicated, where and why the conversation took place, and the time of day or night it was by the clock on the wall. (I'm exaggerating a bit, but you get the point.)

For those like me, we need not forget the incident, but allow it to serve as a red flag to set boundaries (rather than brick walls or barriers) so that a particular offense will not occur again to that magnitude. Choosing to forgive and replace the memory of ill will with a positive thought that incites passion instead of pain will bring healing. I've heard it said that if time was all that we needed to heal, then God would be unnecessary. Of course, we know the latter is untrue. We need God as much as we need the air that we breathe, especially to love those who seem to be unlovable and to forgive those who should be unforgivable if we rely on our human nature alone.

Please know that only the unconditional love of God can work in and through a woman who has been raped or abused to forgive her rapist and abuser. Only the incomprehensible love that flows from above can overshadow the callous coating of a woman's heart who finds it difficult to love and forgive her own self after having an abortion. It takes God's love to prevail in a situation where a woman blames herself for actions of a relative or a person she trusted who molested her as a child. Oh, yes, the love of God is able to cover a multitude of sins and set us free indeed!

Here are scriptures that will assist in learning how to love and forgive others, not for their sake, but for our own, on our journey toward joyful living and holistic health.

Application Principles

1. *God sees and understands our pain and will forgive us and help us to forgive others once we confess that we need His help.* (Psalm 25:18 & 86:5)

2. *The forgiveness we receive from God is in direct proportion to the forgiveness we give to others.* (Matthew 6:12 & 14)

3. *Avoiding judgment and condemnation and choosing to forgive others will cause the same behavior to be reciprocated toward us.* (Luke 6:37)

Where Do I Go From Here?
Accountability and Responsibility
Journaling

- Is there a person in your life who has greatly offended you and needs your forgiveness? If so, whom, and what will you do to begin the process of allowing God's love to flow through you in order to forgive him or her?

  _____

  _____

  _____

  _____

  _____

  _____

- Often times, past experiences have caused so much pain and guilt that it makes it difficult to forgive ourselves. List two steps that you will take in order to leave the past and a victim mentality behind in order to move forward as a victor. Begin the process immediately.

  _____

  _____

  _____

  _____

  _____

- Do you have any controlling behaviors, judgmental attitudes or anything to prove to show someone that you were or are right? If so, honestly admit those areas of concern below and seek God for His help, forgiveness and love so that you can administer it to those who need it the most in your life.

CHAPTER 5

PRACTICING SELF-CARE

"Give yourself a break and take care of your most valuable asset – YOU! Then you can be of service to those who need what you have to offer."
Dr. Natalie A. Francisco

Taking the time to nurture our spiritual, mental, emotional and physical needs is vitally important. I call it *self-care* because it is an intentional focus of the mind, heart and will to do what is necessary to tend to the most valuable asset that God has given us other than His Son Jesus Christ—ourselves. To be quite honest, it occurred to me shortly after my 40th birthday that I had devoted my time and energy into the lives of my husband, children, and the church to make sure that their needs and interests were tended to at the expense of neglecting my own. I really didn't realize how much time I invested in my children until they left for college and, all of a sudden, I experienced a void, and my husband and I were confronted with a time of awkward transition as empty nesters. We didn't realize how much they consumed our time when we were not in church, and how quiet the house would become without them. We are still adjusting now that our oldest has purchased her own home after finishing graduate school, and our middle daughter just recently completed her bachelor's degree, while our youngest is about to enter her junior year of college.

I don't regret literally pouring myself into my family or our ministry, but I do realize that there are things that I would have done differently to develop personal interests outside of my responsibilities as a wife, mother and the many roles I've had in full-time ministry. It dawned on me that I had allowed myself to be swallowed up in the shadows of putting everyone else first, and my health suffered as a result. I had two procedures done—an endometrial ablation and a partial hysterectomy because I had developed fibroids and had a tumor between the size of a very large grapefruit and a soccer ball removed. When my children left for college and to pursue a life on their own, I discovered that I needed to find an outlet that would nurture my intellectual, social and emotional needs that had been lacking. Although I had majored on feeding my spirit, the other components of my four-square development desperately needed attention, and fast! Early pre-menopausal symptoms didn't help the situation either! Is anyone else willing to admit the same?

There are red flags that are raised in our lives in order to get our attention when our four-square fitness level (our spiritual, mental, emotional and physical development) is out of whack. An acronym that Charles Stanley uses serves as a red flag and a personal assessment tool. (Thank you, Dr. Pam Ogletree, my friend, for giving me this information!)

- **H HUNGRY** – This hunger is not physical, but spiritual in nature. If we don't take the time to nourish our spirit, we become apathetic.
- **A ANGRY** – Often, anger is the byproduct of another root cause such as fear, shame or sadness that has never been dealt with and has escalated to another level.
- **L LONELY** – Loneliness is not just the result of being without the company of people. It is possible to feel lonely even in the midst of primary relationships.
- **T TIRED** – Being tired does not imply physical exhaustion alone. Mental weariness and exhaustion can occur from being overworked, overloaded and under-rested.

If any of the symptoms above occur, causing us to feel hungry, angry, lonely or tired, we should view them as red flags and a signal to **H.A.L.T.** or more pointedly, to stop and examine why those symptoms exist and deal with them before a head on collision takes place. Let's say this aloud to drive this point home: *"I must practice self-care!"*

Let us not forget that we can still be productive while we

are experiencing any of the above symptoms, and that God can utilize our experiences as lessons from which we can learn and leave as a legacy for others who look to us for leadership or guidance. God can even utilize hunger, anger, loneliness or tiredness to get our attention. What we are experiencing can be used to:

- Cultivate much needed humility in our lives;
- Build character and strengthen core values within us;
- Identify a state of complacency, lethargy or mediocrity; and/or,
- Shift the season in our lives as we move out of our comfort zone into a new assignment.

Pre- and post-menopausal conditions are real, but neglecting the practice of self-care will only make the conditions worse. The following symptoms occur, not just during menopause as some may be able to attest, but they also are a result of what will happen when our most valuable asset has been ignored:

- An inability to sleep soundly without patterns of interruption;
- An inability to focus for extended periods of time;
- An inability to enjoy routine activities;
- Irritability, frustration and aggravation;
- Unintentional weight loss or weight gain; and
- Uncontrollable crying spells.

I can hear you saying now, *"I need to practice self-care!"*

Once again, let's look at a biblical model that we can follow in order to nurture our four-square development. We'll examine the life of Samuel in the Old Testament and Jesus Christ in the New Testament. Who better to follow than Jesus Himself?

1 Samuel 2:6:

And the child Samuel grew in stature, and in favor both with the LORD and men.

Luke 2:52:

And Jesus increased in wisdom and stature, and in favor with God and men.

Application Principles

1. ***Growth is necessary to prevent complacency and stagnation.*** Hannah's child, Samuel, did not remain a child forever. He was weaned from his mother and prepared for ministry to be mentored by the priest Eli at a very young age. 1 Samuel 2:6 lets us know that Samuel continued to develop in his stature (physique) and in favor with God (his spiritual connection) and man (his social connection). Notice, however, that the mental or intellectual component is not mentioned in this

verse. Any component that is not actively nurtured will become a weak link that can cause the other components to be out-of-balance. Worse yet, any component that ceases to grow can lead to complacency and cause stagnation to set in, and there's nothing worse than the feel and smell of that!

2. *Developing our four-square components should be an ongoing process.* In Luke 2:52, Jesus is the prime example of four-square development which continued on earth until His death, burial and resurrection. The scripture validates that He increased or continued to grow in wisdom (intellect), stature (physical strength), and in favor with God (His spiritual Source) and men (His social network). Other scriptures support the fact that He took time to rest, eat and exercise as He traveled from town to town to ensure that he was in good physical shape. He also fasted, prayed and was ministered to by the Holy Spirit as needed to tend to His spiritual development. He was found in the synagogue as a young child and speaking to multitudes wherever He went, and His inquisitive nature and masterful teaching underscore His intellectual stimulation and growth. And of course, Jesus surrounded Himself with an outer group of 120, an associate group of 70, and a smaller group of 12 disciples (although one betrayed Him, but then again, Jesus chose Judas Iscariot because He

already knew that scriptures concerning His death, burial and resurrection had to be fulfilled). To further reinforce the need for human contact and social growth, Jesus chose a more intimate, inner circle among His disciples who were asked to join Him in prayer and on specific occasions when He wanted to reveal more of Himself to those who knew Him better than anyone else (Peter, James and John). We each need to have an inner circle of trusted friends with whom we can be ourselves without position, platform or pretense.

I must also address issues of mental health that are ignored because of the stigma of what is associated with visiting a psychiatrist, psychologist, counselor or therapist, particularly within the African-American community. Apparently, there are some who think that admitting to the need for or seeking out such help from these professional experts, is the same as admitting that they are "coo-coo" or "crazy," to use the vernacular of our culture. Nothing could be further from the truth.

Because this perception needs to be exposed, more people within leadership roles in our communities, and especially clergy from the pulpit, need to address this taboo subject to remove the stigma and to refer those who need counseling and therapy to those who are professionally trained to offer it for the good of those who need it and those closest to them.

One final issue I'll address regarding the practice of self-care is the importance of having an outlet that distinctly represents our own interests and nurtures any or all of our four-square components. This outlet should be separate from our familial, employment and church responsibilities and relationships. For example, to nurture my spiritual growth, I not only attend church consistently, but outside of church, I spend time with God throughout the day by praying, reading the Bible and other spiritual resources, listening to inspirational music, journaling and blogging to encourage myself and others. I also upload status updates on Facebook and Twitter, and email others using God-inspired thoughts that blend into words that I've read or written myself to bless the lives of other people.

For intellectual growth, I purpose to be a voracious reader of resources that cause me to think critically; to visit museums to learn new information; and to travel to places where I've never been in order to become acculturated and accepting of others' perspectives and ways of doing things. I strive to develop my social life by being intentional about maintaining current friendships and developing new associations with those who can sharpen and stretch me to be better than I am in order to grow and excel, but also so that I won't take myself so seriously. My special sistah-friends as I call them, make me laugh so hard at times that my stomach begins to hurt when we get together because we can be real and free to be ourselves without fear of judgment, criticism or having control over each other.

In an effort to grow in my physical development, I am determined to exercise at least four times a week, and to make wiser choices regarding my food consumption and calorie intake. I am still working on getting at least seven hours of sleep a night, which is harder for me to do because I have become so accustomed to meditating, writing and working when the house is quiet, which is a habit that began when my children were very young. (I'll talk more about how I care for my physical body, particularly in the area of receiving proper rest, in chapter seven.)

And finally, just for relaxation, entertainment and fun, I love getting massages to reduce stress and promote wellness, attending concerts and theatre productions, traveling the world, shopping, and yes, fine dining. It's true—my family and I really do enjoy eating both at home and in restaurants across the country. My husband, oldest daughter, and my sister, Renee`, can see a picture of an entrée, a salad or dessert in a magazine or on the Food Network, prepare it, and present it perfectly to our sheer delight. I just have to eat smaller portions now or burn more calories than I have eaten!

Now that we've covered all of the aforementioned information vital to your inner health and wholeness, don't you feel the need to remind yourself again, out loud, that you must practice self-care? It is an intentional, ongoing effort that requires thought, a strategy, and the willpower to follow through in placing yourself on your "to-do" list daily, without feeling guilty for doing so. If Jesus could do it, you and I certainly can!

Where Do I Go From Here?
Accountability and Responsibility Journaling

- Nurturing the spiritual, mental, physical and social components of our four-square development is a must in order to maintain balance and harmony within and around us. Which area if any, needs to be intentionally cared for in your life, and what steps will you take to ensure that this area is not neglected?

_____

_____

_____

_____

_____

_____

- It is imperative that we seek ongoing growth in our four-square development. List below at least one strategy that you will follow through to experience increase in each area:

Spiritual

_____

_____

_____

Mental/Intellectual

_____

_____

_____

Social

_____

_____

_____

Physical

_____

_____

_____

- Have you ever considered counseling or therapy to deal with difficult issues from an interpersonal perspective (relationship with yourself) or intrapersonal point of view (in your relationships with others)? Why or why not?

_____

_____

_____

_____

_____

_____

_____

- Do you have a hobby that acknowledges and celebrates your own interests? If not, what areas would interest you in order to develop or hone natural talents and skills just for fun?

_____

_____

_____

_____

_____

_____

_____

CHAPTER 6

PRIORITIZING FAMILY & OTHERS

*"When you slow down, you allow the things
that matter most to catch up."*
MARSHAWN EVANS

No matter how successful we are or strive to be in our life's
work, we must remember that our first priority, particularly
for those of us who are married and/or have children, is to
succeed within our homes, and it takes intentional effort
for that to occur. Having a healthy family unit requires
that the roles of husband, wife, and child are understood
and modeled as a core value. Whereas both father and
mother are necessary in the growth and development of a
child, women are intentionally needed to nurture and
inspire the next generation. The world needs men and
women to take their responsibilities seriously within the
home regarding their commitment to model and maintain
a healthy environment that promotes love, learning,
solidarity and strength, particularly when it comes to
husband-wife and parent-child relationships.

There are a diversity of family units that exist in this day and time. It cannot be assumed that there is a two-parent home in the traditional sense with a mother and a father for a myriad of reasons. Single parent homes abound just as there are a number of homes where children may be reared by a grandparent or guardian. Consider these statistics recently released in December 2010 by The Marriage and Religion Research Institute (a project of the Family Research Council):

> More than half of American youth are growing up in families torn apart by divorce, separation and single parenthood. A study by the Marriage and Religion Research Institute reveals that 55 percent of American teenagers are living in non-traditional family structures marred by divorce, separation or unmarried parents. By comparison, 45 percent of young adults live in intact families where the biological parents are married to one another since before or around the time of their child's birth. The "Index of Belonging and Rejection" also reports that African-American and Native American teens are more likely than teens of other races and ethnicities to come up in a broken family. Fewer than one in four American Indian and Alaskan Native adolescents (24 percent) have lived with married biological parents throughout childhood. African-American teens are least likely to live in an intact family. Fewer than one in five (17 percent) live with

married parents. At 62 percent, Asian-American teens are most likely to live with wedded, biological parents. Caucasian teens follow close behind at 54 percent. Lead researcher Pat Fagan said the data displays a change in Americans' concept of family structure.

No matter what kind of family unit or concept of family structure may exist, there should still be a conscientious effort to place the wellbeing of the family ahead of other responsibilities and interests as a core value. Within the context of marriage, husbands and wives should strive to place their relationship with each other, as well as parenting, if applicable, at the top of their priority list. Successful families do not just fall out of the sky or naturally develop. They are a product of determination, diligence, care and concern on the part of individuals committed to having a healthy home environment for the sake of all parties involved.

It is imperative to examine what a healthy family looks like from a biblical perspective, for that is the foundation upon which a Christian family is built. Therefore, the responsibilities of husbands and wives, in their function and relationship toward one another, as well as toward their children, must be understood before they can be modeled.

The Role of a Husband/Father

Men who know how to love and serve God will in turn

know how to love and serve their wives. An example of this can be seen in the first two chapters of Genesis. In the beginning, after God created the heavens and the earth, He then created the pinnacle of His handiwork when He made man. Adam, the first man, was created first and given the responsibility of naming the animals and tending the Garden of Eden as he walked and talked with God in the cool of the day. Notice that man was given the responsibility of work before he was ever given a woman or wife. (Single women, please pay attention to this!) As a result, Adam would learn how to provide for and attend to the needs of his wife because he had a track record of doing so as he practiced with the animals and in the garden. The primary function of a husband within a Christian home then, is to set a godly example in and outside of the home environment by loving God, providing for his household, and honoring his wife by loving, supporting, and valuing her. (For supporting scriptures, please refer to Ephesians 5:25, Colossians 3:19 and I Peter 3:7.)

According to Ephesians 6:4, children thrive in a home where fathers provide godly admonition. Rather than provoking children to become angry and to rebel, fathers are encouraged to rear their children in such a way as to cause them to excel in life. There are three distinct ways in which to do so:

1. Discipline with love, correction and instruction;
2. Give godly fatherly advice as to what to do and what

not to do; and

3. Be your child's parent, not his or her best friend or sibling!

The Role of a Wife/Mother

Nurturing is easier for women to provide because of our "helpmate" nature. When reviewing chapters 1 and 2 of Genesis, once again we can surmise that Adam had completed his assignments after having been given the ability to work and name the animals in the Garden of Eden. Afterwards, God made a declarative statement in His observation of Adam: *"It is not good for man to be alone"* (Genesis 2:18). For that reason, God, as the first anesthesiologist, put Adam to sleep so that He could perform surgery on him. God took Adam's rib, and from it fashioned woman, building her from the inside out with the exact specifications of mind, body and spirit that were needed to complement Adam in any and every comparable way. As such, Eve was to be flexible, adaptable and suitable so that whatever Adam lacked she *would* and *could* become and provide. (Once again, we see that God knew that man needed help and that woman—or the right woman that is—is the answer that he needs.)

Wives are to set the proper tone for a healthy family within the home by loving God, loving and respecting her husband, and ensuring that her household is managed well. Her "helpmate" nature is utilized by providing proper nurture in the following ways:

1. Give tender care and protection to her children for their spiritual and natural growth and development;
2. Motivate her children to love and serve God by her example and their own choice; and
3. Encourage her children to flourish by helping them to discover and use their gifts, talents and abilities.

Placing family relationships at the top of our priority list will help to create balance and minimize the feeling of guilt or regret that may occur because the family has been neglected or placed further down our "to do" list. Friendships, co-workers and associates all have a place in our lives as well, but that place must be identified as those relationships are placed in their proper order. Here are a few scriptures upon which to meditate that include relevant principles in relation to prioritizing our family and others:

Ephesians 6:1-4:

Children, obey your parents in the Lord, for this is right.

"Honor your father and mother," *which is the first commandment with promise:*

"that it may be well with you and you may live long on the earth."

And you, fathers, do not provoke your children to wrath, but bring them up in the training and admonition of the Lord.

Application Principles

1. ***Children must be taught to respect, listen to, and obey their parents because it is the right thing to do.*** Parents are the first representation of authority that children will ever see. In addition, a child's love for and view of God and a relationship with Him (as opposed to just a religious experience), is both seen and learned by the example that parents set within the home. Setting the right tone within a Christian home involves learning, and therefore modeling what is right or pleasing according to God's Word and will, as implied in Ephesians 6:1.

2. ***There is a blessing that accompanies adherence to God's Word for children.*** Verses two and three of Ephesians chapter six stipulate the most important responsibility that children have within the home, and that is to honor their parents. In so doing, there are benefits of blessing that follow, namely that the child will in turn have a blessed life as well as the promise of a long life. Obeying the parents that God has assigned as stewards is a sure way for children to inherit these precious promises.

3. ***The role of the father is to be resident and evident in the life of his child.*** According to Ephesians 6:4, we can understand why there are so many

disheartened, angry children (and women, too). When the father is absent in the life of his child, there will be inevitable, negative repercussions, unless God intervenes. Rather than being an absentee father, or one who does not take his priorities and responsibilities seriously, fathers are encouraged to step up to the plate by providing care, concern, correction, inspiration and instruction. Those are the kind of role models that children, particularly young men, need to see and follow.

Proverbs 17:17:

A friend loves at all times, and a brother is born for adversity.

Proverbs 27:17:

As iron sharpens iron, So a man [woman] sharpens the countenance of his [her] friend.

Application Principles

1. ***True friends have unconditional love for each other in the best and worst of times.*** Proverbs 17:17 reiterates the importance of cultivating growth in the social component of our four-square development. Seeking out and maintaining friendships in primary familial relationships and between "sister-friends" will add to the richness of

our lives in ways that are unexpected and certainly unparalleled. Such genuine friendships, and the relationships between spouses as well as between siblings, can be God-sent when prioritized appropriately and managed well.

2. *The right kind of friend will add value, strength and accountability as a sharpening edge in the relationship.* Just as a knife is sharpened by scraping it against another piece of steel, so a friend becomes sharper spiritually, intellectually, socially and physically by being in the company of one who will bring out the best, the brightest and the brilliance within her. She will begin to grow in leaps and bounds, and so will her friend, because the benefits in such a relationship are mutual. Proverbs 27:17 attests to the truth and power of such a friendship.

Husbands and wives have a responsibility to honor, love and respect each other. Parents and guardians who have children, whether they are single or married, are to make sure that their children are well taken care of, and that their homes are havens of love, laughter, peace, security and stability. Forest E. Witcraft reminds us of what is important in terms of prioritizing what I've learned that really matters most: "A hundred years from now, it will not matter what my bank account was, the sort of house I lived in, or the kind of car I drove. But the world may be different because

I was important in the life of a child."

Generations are depending on us to pass on a legacy to them that will last—a legacy upon which they can build and pass on to succeeding generations. When our family relationships and friendships are nurtured properly and valued appropriately, then our homes, communities, nation and world will benefit greatly.

The information shared in this chapter regarding the prioritization of families and friendships has been practiced and is still a matter that requires my attention and due diligence. Although my husband and I have been married for over twenty-seven years with three adult children, we do not claim to have it all together. Quite frankly, relationships between spouses, parents and their children, and friends, involve a tremendous amount of effort. Refusing to put in the work required simply shows that those relationships are being taken for granted, and the people that should be the most important to us are devalued as a result.

Here are specific suggestions that, if utilized, will help to prioritize and repair damaged relationships changing them into good ones, and transform the good relationships into something even greater:

Additional Suggestions for Prioritizing Family and Friend Relationships

1. Pray for your spouse, child(ren), significant other and special friends and ask them to pray for you.

2. Develop a family vision that requires equal input from both spouses (if applicable), as well as ownership, participation and support from those living within the household.

3. Allow faith in God to be the common thread that fosters unity.

4. Seek to maintain an environment of encouragement and an attitude of appreciation amongst family and friends.

5. Give family members and close friends time and space to be who God created them to be.

6. Refuse to entertain negative thoughts and words from others about those you love.

7. Seek ways to be a blessing to family and friends.

Where Do I Go From Here?
Accountability and Responsibility Journaling

- Think about the people and things that are most important in your life right now. Truthfully list them in the place of priority in which they currently are held in terms of your time and attention.

_____

_____

_____

_____

_____

_____

_____

- After honestly looking at what you've written above, rearrange the relationships, friendships and/or things you've listed in the order that they should be.

_____

_____

_____

_____

_____

_____

_____

- What relationships and areas, if any, do you need to give your attention to in order to foster a healthy home environment?

  _____

  _____

  _____

  _____

  _____

  _____

  _____

- According to Proverbs 27:17, do you have friends in your life who add value, strength, a sharpening edge and accountability? If so, name them below. If not, what will you do to be that kind of friend as well as to attract such a friend into your life?

  _____

  _____

  _____

  _____

  _____

  _____

  _____

Outer Health & Wholeness

CHAPTER 7

R-E-S-P-E-C-T/T.C.B.
(I Must Respect and Take Care of My Body)

"I always felt that my greatest asset was not my physical ability; it was my mental ability."
BRUCE JENNER

Bruce Jenner's face has appeared on the Wheaties cereal box because he is a beloved American athlete and came to be known as an Olympic champion many times over. As physically adept as he was (and still seems to be at his age), he attributes his greatest strength to his mental acumen as stated in the aforementioned quote. I find his statement most provocative because it reiterates something that my husband conveyed to our congregation in one of his sermons:

"Everything begins with a thought."

—Bishop L. W. Francisco III

It is interesting to note that everything that God created first began as a mere thought before coming into existence. Proverbs 8:22-31 emphasizes that wisdom existed before the heavens and the earth were formed. Isn't that a powerful thought to consider? If we were to apply that as a principle in our lives, we could surmise that anything that we desire to accomplish must first be seen as a mental image upon the canvas of our minds before we can expect to see it physically. That means that we have the power within us right now to think and create, and therefore, to act accordingly to bring it to fruition. Wow!

I realized that the power to imagine and create the kind of body that I wanted, along with the energy that I needed, was within my grasp all along, but I was not acting upon it...until I decided to "R-E-S-P-E-C-T ... find out what it means to me!" It was time to "take care of TCB," as Aretha Franklin would sing, but the TCB I needed to concern myself with was learning how to respect and take care of my body. The decision to do so began in October of 2009 with a mere thought!

During the second weekend of October, I host an annual Women of Worth & Worship conference at Calvary Community Church in Hampton, VA. A few weeks before my conference in 2009, my sistah-friends, Sujay, CJ and I decided to rendezvous in Nassau at The Atlantis Resort where Sujay was hosting her Women in Ministry International Conference. The plan was for us to enjoy a personal vacation together after the conference had ended. I flew immediately after my conference ended that Sunday to Nassau and was so wiped out that I fell asleep sitting up in the chair of my hotel room instead of in the bed. My energy had been zapped, not just because I had a full conference weekend as the host, worship leader, choir director and speaker, but also because I was significantly overweight.

I'll never forget the day that the three of us were sitting on the pristine sandy beach of The Atlantis Royal Towers Resort playing in the sand as we joyfully took in the beauty of the emerald green and aqua blue Caribbean waters. It was truly a well deserved time of getting away and enjoying each other's company and sisterhood. We then proceeded to the pool area where we each took our royal positions in the well appointed chaise lounges overlooking the cascading pool. Because we were (and are) friends who also sharpen one another, we made a pact to check on one another from time to time and to encourage each other to make healthier choices regarding our bodies. We dared each other to call or text with the amount of weight we had lost or some sort of progress report regarding our new pact and decision to be "fit, fine and fabulous" by the same time the following year for our October conferences. The challenge was on, and it began with a thought and the ability to be accountable to one another.

CJ had to leave to return to Texas the next day, but Sujay and I had an extra day of vacation planned, and we began it early by deciding to work out in Atlantis' well equipped fitness center. Before taking our places respectively on the treadmill and elliptical, we decided to weigh in—something I hadn't done in years. I was utterly shocked and devastated to learn that I weighed a whopping 232 lbs! I had never weighed that much in my life, not even when I was at what I thought would have been my heaviest weight at 216 pounds after my first child was born. The challenge was on for real!

From that day in October 2009 until the day of this book's publishing, I have lost approximately 60 pounds without the use of diet pills or dieting period. I used what was at my disposal all along: wisdom, willpower, discipline, and an accountability system. Since so many people asked me to share my weight loss secrets, I decided to include them in this book. This has indeed been an incredible part of my personal journey towards joyful living and holistic health. There are essentially ten successful steps that enabled me to reach my goal of having better blood pressure readings, being released from having to take blood pressure medication by my physician, and giving away and auctioning off all of my former clothes for the benefit of our WOWW conference charities. I am now wearing my desired size ten dream clothes that I purchased to reward myself, and it all began with, as Bruce Jenner stated, the greatest asset that you and I possess—mental ability.

Step 1: Create a mental image of your new desired body. Too often we focus on the way things are in our life right now, without giving much thought to the way things can and should be and devising a strategy to get us there. One of the best things I did to jump start my weight loss success was to see myself the way I wanted to look, dress, and feel so that I could function at an optimum level. The power of meditation in this sense is incredible, for it affects both the conscious and the subconscious mind and allows the body to operate in alignment with what the mind sees and believes.

Step 2: Determine to do only what you can continue for the rest of your life. It was important to set myself up to succeed. I decided that whatever I chose to do in terms of eating and exercising would be something that I could follow through with and learn to enjoy for the rest of my life. I knew that I didn't want to start and stop any diet plan, because I've never liked diets in the first place, especially since the first three letters of the word diet are d-i-e and I didn't plan on dying anytime soon. I also knew that the exercise routine that I began had to be believable to me and therefore achievable. I've never been a runner, so jogging at any pace never crossed my mind. I could, however, use my *Walk-Away-The-Pounds DVD* with Leslie Sansone and the exercise equipment already set up in my home gym. I just needed to activate my willpower and use wisdom (good ole' common sense) to pace myself and to be consistent.

Step 3: Choose an accountability partner and let them know of your progress and regress. It is always easier to exercise with someone else or even with a group, but that isn't always feasible. My husband and I tried to be accountable to each other in a weight loss and exercise plan in the past, but it was short-lived because it was too easy to sabotage each other since we both love to eat great food at any time on any given day, and just about anywhere! Since that didn't work, I knew I needed to choose another accountability partner if I really wanted to succeed, and that I also needed to have discipline to follow through alone if and when necessary. My closest friends live out of state, so we couldn't exercise together, but we could serve as accountability partners for the sake of checking in to encourage one another, especially during those times when instead of moving forward, we moved backwards by falling off the weight wagon because perfect conditions do not exist. Having someone to share successes and failures with provides much needed support which should be mutually beneficial.

Step 4: Choose a system to record food choices, exercise routines and weight that works best for you. My husband told me about a wonderful application on his iPad that I could also download on my iPod Touch, and it was F-R-E-E! The app is called *Lose It! version 3.5.0, © 2008-2010 by FitNow, Inc.* The program allows me to easily enter and edit food items, exercises, my daily weight and goal weight. Based on the information entered, the program will compute how many calories are budgeted daily based on the number of pounds I want to lose weekly

(½, 1, 1 ½ or no more than 2 lbs) to reach my goal weight. The app calculates the expected date when I will reach my goal to keep me on track, and also lets me know if I'm under or over my allotted calories once food and exercise data has been entered for the day. This accountability system has been wonderful in helping me to create and maintain good, healthy habits in making wiser food choices and exercising regularly.

Step 5: Commit to burning more calories than you consume with consistent cardiovascular and strength training exercises. Since I purposed not to deprive myself of all the foods I like because I despise diets, I make sure that I burn off more calories than I eat in order to lose the weight I need to lose to stay on track. I began my commitment to respect and take care of my body in October 2009 by implementing an exercise regimen consisting of at least 30 minutes of cardio and strength training for my upper body (biceps, triceps, deltoid and chest muscles) and lower body (abdomen/oblique, quadriceps, hamstring and calf muscles) using 3, 5 and 10 lb free weights three times a week. My cardio consisted of working out on the elliptical, the stationary bike or with Leslie Sansone's *Walk-Away-The-Pounds DVD*. I have now increased my workout from 3 to at least 4-5 times a week, and my body both craves and loves it!

Step 6: Drink plenty of water and limit sodas, caffeine and alcoholic beverages. Oh, how I love water! I decided to replace sodas and drink plenty of this life giving substance after finding out from a physician that my mother died from colon cancer, a disease that is totally preventable and curable if caught early enough, because she refused to drink water. According to an internet website source (www.shapefit.com/water-benefits.html), "the human body, which is made up of between 55 and 75 percent water (lean people have more water in their bodies because muscle holds more water than fat), is in need of constant water replenishment." It is recommended that we consume at least eight 8 oz. glasses of water a day. When we do, we can look forward to these benefits of drinking water: weight loss; relief of headaches and back pains; youthful and healthy skin; better productivity at work; more energy; help with digestion and constipation; less cramps and strains; decreased likelihood of becoming ill; relief of fatigue; a better mood; and a reduced risk of bladder and colon cancer. (For more information, visit www.mangosteen-natural-remedies.com/benefits-of-drinking-water.html.)

Step 7: Eat three balanced meals per day with healthy snacks in between to boost your metabolism. I have heard it said that we should eat breakfast like a king (the first and biggest meal of the day), lunch like a prince (a medium sized mid-day meal) and dinner like a pauper (the smallest meal of the evening). Eating meals consistently with small snacks in between such as fruit, almonds, trail mix, granola or 100 calorie snack packs, will speed up our metabolism as opposed to slowing it down as a result of meals being skipped. Our new body will thank us for it!

Step 8: Discipline yourself to implement a cut-off time to prohibit late night eating. Years ago, late night eating, caused painful and almost unbearable heartburn and indigestion. I would have to sleep upright in the bed because it hurt too much to lie down. All I needed to do, once again, was to initiate common sense and activate my will power to make a change. It has been said that doing the same thing over and over and expecting different results is the definition of insanity. My heartburn and indigestion stopped when I began to do something different: I decided not to eat after seven p.m. except for special, scheduled functions. This one change alone aided in dramatic weight loss as well.

Step 9: Get the proper amount of rest. I must admit that I am still working on this step, simply because my most creative thoughts and accompanying spurts of energy occur at night. (When ideas come to my mind, particularly in the evening hours, I move on them quickly.) The ideal amount of sleep to get is between 7-9 hours per night. Older individuals may find it useful to take a power nap during the day as well—a beauty secret from actress Sophia Loren and my mother-in-law, Naomi Francisco, who are 75 and 76 years old respectively and full of youthful energy. I, too, feel well-rested and prepared for the day when I've received at least 8 hours of sleep the night before.

Step 10: Adjust your weight loss or maintenance goals accordingly as needed. It is perfectly fine to plan for days when we will eat the desserts we desire, the breads and pastries we enjoy, and the pasta dishes we adore. It is worse to deprive ourselves, binge on everything in sight, and then not reach our weight loss goals at all because we have overtly or covertly sabotaged our own success. Adjusting our plans along the way will require devising and following through with a strategy to burn off excess calories consumed by increasing our exercise regimen as well as by decreasing the portions of food we eat the next day or so until we get back on track.

There are two scriptural passages related to the care of the body that will certainly assist in the pursuit of healthier lifestyle choices. Consider the following:

Romans 12:1-2:

> *I beseech you therefore, brethren, by the mercies of God, that you present your bodies a living sacrifice, holy, acceptable to God,* which is *your reasonable service.*
>
> *And do not be conformed to this world, but be transformed by the renewing of your mind, that you may prove what is that good and acceptable and*

perfect will of God.

1 Timothy 4:8:

For bodily exercise profits a little, but godliness is profitable for all things, having promise of the life that now is and of that which is to come.

Application Principles

1. **God is pleased when our bodies are holy and healthy.** Romans chapter 12, verse 1, urges us to think of our bodies as an offering presented to God. In return, God will help us to make wiser decisions for a holier and healthier lifestyle if we so desire. It is the least we can do as our response for His loving kindness toward us.

2. **In order to create new habits and see positive results, our minds must be renewed.** Romans chapter 12, verse 2 lets us know that there are two systems that will guide our behavior based on which one we choose: the world's system and God's system. In order to experience a better quality of life in all respects, our belief system cannot be conformed to the world's way of doing things, but rather, it must be transformed and influenced by the principles of God's Word. Thoughts determine actions, and actions, once they become consistent,

determine habits.

3. ***Caring for our body and spirit are important.*** 1 Timothy 4:8 lets us know that although we gain a little profit from bodily exercise, a godly lifestyle is beneficial in every way. However, we will still benefit as needed from our choice to take care of our body, which houses our spirit and mind.

Our bodies are to be offered to God as instruments of righteousness (right or holy living), and doing so entails making right choices regarding the treatment of our bodies. When we truly love ourselves, we'll make wiser decisions for the sake of living a healthier lifestyle and gaining the benefits that are sure to manifest as a result. Implementing the ten successful steps shared in this chapter helped me to reach my healthy lifestyle goals, which included losing sixty lbs within a year, without the use of a personal trainer, diet pills, or a diet of any kind, and being released from a prescribed blood pressure medication. Wisdom, willpower, discipline and an accountability system are essential keys needed to *R-E-S-P-E-C-T* and *Take Care* of our *Bodies*.

Where Do I Go From Here?
Accountability and Responsibility Journaling

- Do you respect your body enough to take care of it better? If so, what strategy will you implement in regards to better eating and exercising habits? Write the details of your healthier lifestyle strategy below and include a time frame.

_____

_____

_____

_____

_____

_____

_____

- Who will you choose as your accountability partner to help you stay on track with your healthier lifestyle strategy listed above?

_____

_____

_____

_____

_____

_____

_____

- Write down the details of the new you according to the image that you create and meditate upon in your mind. Be sure to include how you look and feel, as well as the benefits that you will gain as a result of implementing your healthier lifestyle strategy (i.e., more energy, better blood pressure reading, decreased stress level, new wardrobe, etc.).

Outer Health & Wholeness

CHAPTER 8

MANAGING MY LIFE'S TIME AND MISSION

"Believe in something big. Our life is worth a noble motive."
WALTER ANDERSON

When our nation commemorated the 40th anniversary of the death of Rev. Dr. Martin Luther King, Jr. in 2008, several media clips were replayed to remind us of his life's accomplishments in leading America's Civil Rights Movement, garnering a Nobel Peace Prize, and utilizing nonviolent principles to stand up against social injustice and inhumane treatment. He courageously used his oratorical skills to serve mankind and to share the message of equity and equality on behalf of those who were in fact disenfranchised and marginalized by the hypocrisy and bigotry of society. Dr. King boldly served in the face of what seemed to be insurmountable opposition, impending danger and inevitable death. Coretta Scott King, when asked by her father at one point to come home with him after the King's house had been bombed by hatemongers, decided rather to stay behind and stand with her husband.

Even shortly after her husband's assassination on April 4, 1968, this queen of a woman with the intestinal fortitude and unmitigated gall of a "King" stood with the same striking sanitation workers whom her husband had previously led in a march consisting of 6,000 protestors just a few days before his death.

All of us may not have the academic acumen and oratory prowess that Rev. Dr. Martin Luther King, Jr., possessed, or the scholastic and social graces that Mrs. Coretta Scott King embodied, but each of us does have a unique, God-given gift, talent or ability to make an indelible mark upon our world by believing in something bigger than ourselves. That belief will guide us in discerning our life's mission, which should include the noble and necessary mandate of serving others and not just ourselves.

Corporate and nonprofit entities often have mission statements consisting of core values or principles that guide business practices and the service (or promise) that its target audience of owners and customers expect. In like manner, we should have a personal mission statement that guides our behavior and delivers a promise of serving those in our sphere of influence. That mission becomes our life's charge or work, not just because we've chosen to do it, but because we sense that it is what we are called and equipped by God to accomplish for the sake of pleasing Him and being a blessing to other people.

In an excerpt of his speech entitled *The Drum Major Instinct*, the Rev. Dr. Martin Luther King, Jr. declares emphatically the importance of serving others as a natural part of our life's mission:

> "If you want to be important, wonderful. If you want to be recognized, wonderful! If you want to be great, wonderful! But recognize that he who is greatest among you shall be your servant. That's a new definition of GREATNESS…by giving that definition of GREATNESS, it means that everybody can be great, because everybody can serve. You don't have to have a college degree to serve. You don't have to make your subject and verb agree to serve. You don't have to know about Plato and Aristotle to serve. You don't have to know Einstein's Theory of Relativity to serve. You don't have to know the Second Theory of Thermodynamics in physics to serve. You only need a heart full of grace, a soul generated by love and you can be a servant."

We are all given the same amount of time—24 hours a day—in which to love and serve God, and to love and serve our neighbors as we do ourselves. That is our life's mission. However, our mission and the time we have in which to live it must be managed wisely. There are three verses of scripture in the King James Version that emphasize the importance of managing our life's time and mission:

Ecclesiastes 3:1:

To every [thing there is] a season, and a time to every purpose under the heaven.

Ecclesiastes 8:5:

Whoso keepeth the commandment shall feel no evil thing: and a wise man's heart discerneth both time and judgment.

Colossians 4:5:

Walk in wisdom toward them that are without, redeeming the time.

Application Principles

1. ***Discern the season for doing what needs to be done.*** Identifying priorities, setting goals, and giving those goals and priorities places in our daily schedule will ensure that our life's mission is fulfilled in the right season and at the right time.

2. ***Create a time management plan.*** Writing down our life's mission or vision and setting a time frame for accomplishing specific goals diminishes the likelihood of forgetting important details.

3. ***Allow purpose to unfold each day by using a planner.*** It is a good idea to complete our planner

before going to bed each night. Beginning each day with an agenda and devising a system to use in order to operate our plan helps us to be effective and efficient.

4. *Align our heart, mind, and will with what needs to be accomplished daily.* The agreement of these three components working synergistically will produce benefits when used to operate our time management plan. These benefits include decreased time spent on decision-making and procrastination; decreased crisis; God-inspired direction; increased productivity; and increased quality of work.

5. *We must work our plan well.* It is important to keep all of the information necessary for the purpose of planning and implementing our time management plan in one integrated system. Using the latest technology of a smart phone such as a Blackberry or iPhone, the available apps and program conveniences of an iPod Touch or an iPad, a laptop computer, or simply a planner with a daily calendar, will help tremendously in maintaining consistency in keeping a schedule. It is best to have a portable system at our disposal to prioritize daily task lists, projects, appointments, assignments, travel, etc.

6. *Use wisdom to differentiate between what is urgent,*

what is important, and what should be delegated.
Urgent things take priority over what is important
and should be placed on the top of a daily task list.
Priorities must be set in terms of what needs to be
completed first, and follow in descending order.
Tasks that should be delegated to someone else will
only waste the precious resource of time that God
has given to us. Overload is due to a lack of
discipline and a lack of delegation, perhaps due to
lacking confidence in others to perform. Being
overloaded robs us of our time.

7. *Redeem lost time by making good use of every opportunity.* Time is one vital resource that can never return once it has gone. We must guard our time and use it wisely by seizing each opportunity that comes our way to do good and to serve others, while remembering to place ourselves on the list of those who need to be served or cared for. We cannot bless others if we are not blessed ourselves, nor can we give to others what we do not have.

8. *Assign a time limit to every task/priority daily.* Developing a time log for each activity, event, phone call, meeting and/or goal, will help us and others to respect our time. It helps to focus our concentration on the priority to be accomplished and to determine not to be distracted. By doing so, we show a commitment to value time while

resisting the temptation to waste it.

The word *time* is mentioned 620 times in 523 different verses throughout the King James Version of the Bible. The fact that this tiny yet expansive word is used so many times alludes to its importance and value. Time is appointed and apportioned accordingly by God to us as a matter of stewardship to be managed wisely. It is a precious gift that arrives with the dawning of each new day.

Creating and utilizing a time management plan requires decision, discipline, and determination. Time management is really management of our life's mission as we utilize wisdom to manage the priorities, events and affairs in our lives. Determining to be good stewards of God's time afforded to us, empowers us with the ability to have control over what we do next. Our ability to distinguish between what is urgent and important and to remove unimportant tasks from our schedule, will cause us to be fruitful and fulfilled rather than frustrated and fatigued as we manage our life's time and mission. Pure joy will fill our hearts and flow to others when we believe in and serve a purpose that becomes, as Walter Anderson stated, "a noble motive."

Where Do I Go From Here?
Accountability and Responsibility Journaling

- Time is the resource of God's gift given to us so that we can fulfill our life's mission and manage it well. What do you consider to be your life's mission? What gifts, talents, and abilities do you possess to support and fulfill your life's mission?

  _____

  _____

  _____

  _____

  _____

  _____

  _____

- Identify the "time wasters" in your life below. What can you do to eliminate them, and when will you begin?

  _____

  _____

  _____

  _____

  _____

  _____

  _____

- Do you have a time management plan (TMP) that you utilize on your smart phone, iPod Touch, iPad or personal computer? What will you do to implement a TMP, or if you already have one, how can you become more efficient and effective in utilizing it?

_____

_____

_____

_____

_____

_____

What Impacted Me the Most

SUMMARY

A REALITY CHECK

We have covered a great deal of valuable information learned from and lived through my life experiences, but most of all, derived from the surety of biblical principles that will never lead us astray. All that I have learned could not be contained in this one book. However, the eight chapters that were written encapsulate the successful steps towards a journey for joyful living and holistic health in the four-square development of our spiritual, intellectual/mental, social, and spiritual growth.

This is not a book that can be read quickly and put to the side. Rather, it is a manual for success that can be a lifelong tool for personal assessment as it relates to healthy living in every area of your life. I challenge you to review the chapters that speak to whatever season of life you may be in as often as necessary, and to keep a journal or accountability system (i.e., smart phone, iPad, iPod Touch, laptop, or a notebook) close by to chronicle the ebbs and flows, highs and lows of your journey toward holistic health. Remember that perfect conditions do not and will not exist, but that excellence is certainly attainable with the combination of wisdom, willpower, discipline and of course, an accountability system or partner.

After reviewing the chapters of this book, which one(s) do you really need to focus on right now for maximum impact? Review that chapter as necessary and write down the principles that you've learned or need to apply immediately, as well as your strategy for moving forward. Today is the first day of your new life and the new you. Here is to your own health and wealth for God's glory, your enjoyment, and others' benefit. You WILL succeed!

_____

_____

_____

_____

_____

_____

_____

_____

_____

_____

_____

_____

ABOUT
DR. NATALIE A. FRANCISCO

Dr. Natalie A. Francisco has served as co-pastor of Calvary Community Church and co-founder of Calvary Christian Academy in Hampton, VA, alongside her husband, Bishop L. W. Francisco III. She has also served extensively in full-time ministry for over 26 years in areas of leadership in both the Music and Arts and Christian Education departments of her local church. The culmination of her years of experience in relating to women and children of all ages have been instrumental in affording her the opportunity to author three books: *Wisdom for Women of Worth & Worship: Lessons for a Life of Virtue, Value & Victory*; *Parenting and Partnering with Purpose: Linking Homes, Schools and Churches to Educate Our Children*; and *A Woman's Journal for Joyful Living: Successful Steps to Holistic Health* (all published by St. Paul Press).

As founder and executive director of the Women of Worth Conference and the Women of Worth and Worship Institute (WOWWI), Dr. Francisco seeks to provide godly and practical instruction to women who desire to learn and implement biblical truths and principles from her life's lessons. As a personal mentor and a consultant, she strives to equip others to excel in the areas of ministry, daily living and education. This is accomplished via her books, conferences, seminars, retreats, and several eight-week sessions held throughout the year on location as requested as well as online for registered participants across the country and around the world.

With over fifteen years of television experience alongside her husband, Dr. Francisco also is a contributor to the Shaping Families radio broadcast sponsored by Third Way Media. She offers pastoral insight and biblical solutions while addressing difficult, real life issues that families often face. The broadcast is aired weekly on thirteen radio stations nationwide and can also be heard online. Additionally, Dr. Francisco serves as director on various community and financial services boards, and as an advisory board member of Wisdom Women Worldwide founded by Dr. Suzan Johnson Cook.

Although Dr. Francisco has served as a motivational speaker, teacher, worship leader and author, her greatest joys are found in serving God, spending time with her family and friends, and practicing self-care.

CONTACT
DR. NATALIE A. FRANCISCO

To register for a Women of Worth & Worship session offered onsite or online which includes eight-week sessions with intensive teaching utilizing any or all of her books (*Wisdom for Women of Worth and Worship*, *Parenting and Partnering with Purpose* and *A Woman's Journal for Joyful Living*) as the curriculum guide:

> Dr. Natalie A. Francisco
> Women of Worth & Worship, LLC
> 2311 Tower Place
> Hampton, VA 23666
> Via email: wowwi@nataliefrancisco.com

To visit the Women of Worth & Worship, LLC website:
> www.nataliefrancisco.com

To request Dr. Natalie A. Francisco for church, educational or corporate speaking engagements, conferences, consultations or workshops:

Dr. Natalie A. Francisco
Calvary Community Church
2311 Tower Place
Hampton, VA 23666
(757) 825-1133 ext. 200
Email: wowwi@calvarycommunity.org
Website: www.calvarycommunity.org

To visit Dr. Francisco's book websites:
www.awomansjournalforjoyfulliving.com
www.wisdomforwomenofworthandworship.com
www.parentingandpartneringwithpurpose.com

Made in the USA
Charleston, SC
10 March 2011